Sara Swan Miller

Waterfowl

From Swans to Screamers

Franklin Watts - A Division of Grolier Publishing
New York • London • Hong Kong • Sydney • Danbury, Connecticut

For Jean, Jack, John, Debbie, and Robbie
The Connecticut Swans

Photographs ©: Animals Animals: 27 (Darek Karp), 7 (Robert Maier), 19 (Joe McDonald), 31 (Ronald I. Orenstein), 43 (Maresa Pryor); BBC Natural History Unit: 5 top left (Nigel Bean), 6 (Niall Benvie), 5 top right (John Cancalosi), 1 (Jeff Foott), 41 (David Kjaer); ENP Images: cover, 5 bottom left (Gerry Ellis), 39 (Steve Gettle); Photo Researchers: 21 (Kenneth W. Fink), 42 (William H. Mullins), 23 (Roger Wilmshurst); Tony Stone Images: 29 (Gavriel Jecan), 37 (Neal Mishler); Visuals Unlimited: 25, 33 (John Geriach), 5 bottom right (Ken Lucas), 35 (McCutcheon); Wildlife Collection: 17 (Martin Harvey), 14, 15 (Henry H. Holdsworth), 13 (Gary Schultz).

Illustrations by Jose Gonzales and Steve Savage

Visit Franklin Watts on the Internet at:
http://publishing.grolier.com

Library of Congress Cataloging-in-Publication Data

Miller, Sara Swan.
Waterfowl: from swans to screamers / Sara Swan Miller.
     p. cm. — (Animals in order)
    Includes bibliographical references and index.
    Summary: Describes some members of the waterfowl order, which includes swans, geese, ducks, and screamers.
    ISBN 0-531-11584-4 (lib. bdg.)   0-531-16403-9 (pbk.)
    1. Anatidae—Juvenile literature. [1. Waterfowl. 2. Ducks. 3. Geese. 4. Swans.] I. Title.
II. Series.
    QL696.A52M537   1999
    598.4'1—dc21   98-8204
                                                    CIP
                                                    AC

© 1999 Franklin Watts, A Division of Grolier Publishing
All rights reserved. Published simultaneously in Canada.
Printed in the United States of America.
1 2 3 4 5 6 7 8 9 10 R 08 07 06 05 04 03 02 01 00 99

GROLIER
PUBLISHING

Contents

Wonderful Waterfowl

The word "waterfowl" is used to describe a group, or *order*, of birds that includes ducks, geese, swans, and screamers. Waterfowl are among the most popular of all birds. Even people who aren't interested in bird-watching enjoy watching ducks *dabbling* in a pond and are thrilled by the sight of a flock of geese flying south.

Our interest in waterfowl is nothing new. People have been drawing and painting these birds since the dawn of history. For thousands of years, people have also eaten adult waterfowl and their eggs. We use their *down* to make warm jackets and to stuff pillows and bedcovers.

Look at the four waterfowl on the next page. What do you think they all have in common?

Mallard duck

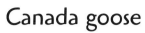

Canada goose

Mute swan

Southern screamer

Traits of the Waterfowl

It's not easy to tell why the waterfowl are all in the same order, unless you're an *ornithologist* (or-nuh-THAWL-uh-jist)—a scientist who studies birds. To decide whether two birds are closely related, ornithologists compare their skeletons and the roofs of their mouths. They also pay attention to how the birds' feathers grow.

By looking carefully at ducks, geese, swans, and screamers, scientists can tell that they have more in common with one another than with other types of birds. This means that all of the birds in the waterfowl order have a common ancestor that lived millions of years ago. Over time, each type of waterfowl has changed in ways that suit their different *habitats* and lifestyles.

A duck's legs are set back on its body.

Waterfowl that spend a lot of time on the water are shaped sort of like a rowboat. The bodies of ducks and swans are wide and flat on the bottom. Their legs are set back on their bodies. That is why these birds are slow and awkward when they walk on land, but strong and quick when they swim in the water.

Waterfowl that spend most of their time on land look different. The legs of geese and screamers are closer to the middle of their bodies. These birds can stand upright and walk easily. The screamers, which look more like turkeys than ducks, have very long toes that allow them to walk on floating plants.

Different waterfowl eat different kinds of foods. Some eat fish, while others eat shellfish, crayfish, and water insects. Still others prefer to eat plants. Almost all waterfowl eat insects.

Some waterfowl, such as geese, do most of their feeding on land. They eat young grasses and other plants or pick up seeds and corn kernels in fields. Many waterfowl feed on water-plants. Some skim their food from the surface of the water. Others tip themselves over—with their high tails in the air—and eat plants that grow underwater. The waterfowl certainly have a variety of lifestyles!

A goose's legs are closer to the center of its body.

The Order of Living Things

A tiger has more in common with a house cat than with a daisy. A true bug is more like a butterfly than a jellyfish. Scientists arrange living things into groups based on how they look and how they act. A tiger and a house cat belong to the same group, but a daisy belongs to a different group.

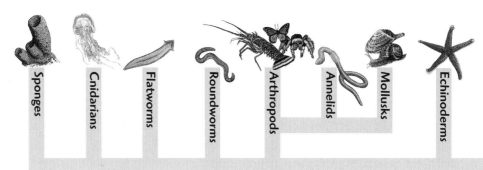

Sponges | Cnidarians | Flatworms | Roundworms | Arthropods | Annelids | Mollusks | Echinoderms

Animals

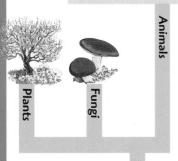

Plants | Fungi

Protists

Monerans

All living things can be placed in one of five groups called *kingdoms*: the plant kingdom, the animal kingdom, the fungus kingdom, the moneran kingdom, or the protist kingdom. You can probably name many of the creatures in the plant and animal kingdoms. The fungus kingdom includes mushrooms, yeasts, and molds. The moneran and protist kingdoms contain thousands of living things that are too small to see without a microscope.

8

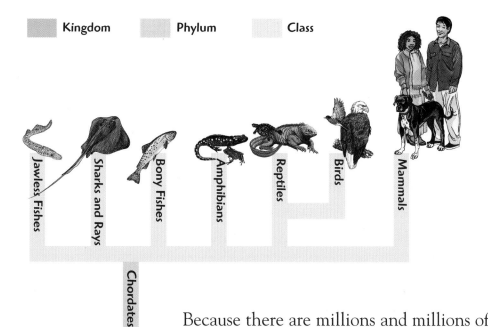

Because there are millions and millions of living things on Earth, some of the members of one kingdom may not seem all that similar. The animal kingdom includes creatures as different as tarantulas and trout, jellyfish and jaguars, salamanders and sparrows, elephants and earthworms.

To show that an elephant is more like a jaguar than an earthworm, scientists further separate the creatures in each kingdom into more specific groups. The animal kingdom can be divided into nine *phyla*. Humans belong to the chordate phylum. Almost all chordates have a backbone.

Each phylum can be subdivided into many *classes*. Humans, mice, and elephants all belong to the mammal class. Each class can be further divided into orders; orders into *families*, families into *genera*, and genera into *species*. All the members of a species are very similar.

How Waterfowl Fit In

You can probably guess that waterfowl belong to the animal kingdom. They have much more in common with spiders and snakes than with maple trees and morning glories.

Waterfowl belong in the chordate phylum. Almost all chordates have a backbone and a skeleton. Can you think of other chordates? Examples include elephants, mice, snakes, frogs, fish, and whales.

All birds belong to the same class. There are about thirty different orders of birds. Waterfowl—ducks, swans, geese, and screamers—make up one of these orders.

Waterfowl are divided into a number of different families and genera. These groups can be broken down into hundreds of species that live on every continent except Antarctica. No matter where you live, you can enjoy watching waterfowl. In this book, you will learn more about fifteen different species of waterfowl.

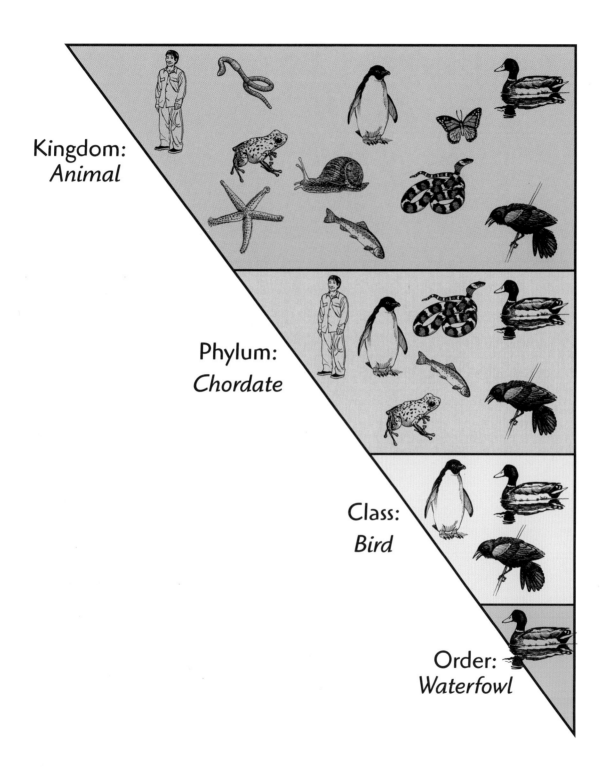

Kingdom: *Animal*

Phylum: *Chordate*

Class: *Bird*

Order: *Waterfowl*

Geese

FAMILY: Anatidae
COMMON EXAMPLE: Snow goose
GENUS AND SPECIES: *Chen caerulescens*
SIZE: 28 inches (70 cm)

In the summer, snow geese can be found far north in the Arctic *tundra*. They spend most of their time wandering over the land or splashing through shallow water in search of food. They're hunting for whatever leaves, seeds, and roots they can find.

Snow geese really like each other's company! They flock together by the hundreds, even in breeding season when most birds would rather be alone. You can hear them barking to each other like little dogs, "Bow-wow! Howk-howk! Bow-wow!"

After mating, the female looks for a safe nesting spot on a small hill. From there, she can watch for foxes and other enemies. She lays her eggs, and about 3 weeks later they hatch. In just a few hours, the young *goslings* are *pattering* about in search of food. Their parents stay nearby to guard them.

Summers are short in the Arctic, so there's not a lot of time to raise goslings. Luckily, the summer days are very long. This gives the goslings extra time to *forage* for food. By the time they are 6 or 7 weeks old, they have grown flight feathers. Now they're ready for the long *migration* south. Some snow geese travel as far south as Mexico! Sometimes, they fly so high that you can barely see them.

Swans

FAMILY: Anatidae
COMMON EXAMPLE: Trumpeter swan
GENUS AND SPECIES: *Cygnus buccinator*
SIZE: 58 1/2 to 72 inches (149 to 183 cm)

A pair of beautiful trumpeter swans glides gracefully over a pond. The still water reflects their bright white feathers. The birds scoop up water plants from the water as they swim along. When they come to deeper water, they tip themselves over, so that their tails are high in the air. The swans can reach plants on the bottom of the pond by stretching their long necks straight down.

Most swans mate for life. Each year, the pair returns to the same shallow pond to raise their young *cygnets*. Sometimes they even come back to the same nest. The male swan helps the female build or repair a nest on a small island in the pond. After the female has laid the eggs, the male

takes turns sitting on them so that the female can feed. When the cygnets are born, both parents take care of the young swans and show them the best feeding sites. The cygnets grow quickly during the summer months. In late fall, when the pond begins to freeze, the whole family flies south with other swans.

In the 1930s these beautiful swans were nearly *extinct*. But now they are protected by law, and trumpeter swans grace our ponds and marshes once more.

Ducks

FAMILY: Anatidae
COMMON EXAMPLE: Wood duck
GENUS AND SPECIES: *Aix sponsa*
SIZE: 17 to 20 inches (43 to 51 cm)

A male wood duck is a very handsome creature. His feathers shine with greens, purples, blues, and bright white. His mate, though, is grayish and drab. Can you guess which one sits on the eggs and raises the ducklings? The female's coloring blends with her surroundings to help keep her, and her young, safe from *predators*.

Wood ducks live around shallow ponds and marshes that are surrounded by woodlands. The females make their nests in tree holes, or in nesting boxes that people have built for them. Some nests are as much as 60 feet (18 m) above the ground!

Because these ducks build nests in tree holes, they can live in areas without much ground cover. But living that high up can be scary for young ducklings. The morning after they hatch, each duckling peers out of the entrance to the nest. For long moments, the ducks teeter there, getting up their courage. Finally, each one takes the plunge. The young ducks leap out, flutter their useless little wings, and land with a splash in the water far below.

In the early 1900s, wood ducks were in danger of extinction. For many years, people had been cutting down their woodland homes

and hunting them for food. Today, laws protect wood ducks, and many people are working to save them. Happily, wood duck populations are thriving once again.

Screamers

FAMILY: Anhimidae
COMMON EXAMPLE: Southern screamer
GENUS AND SPECIES: *Chauna torquata*
SIZE: 36 inches (91 cm)

Screamers don't look or act like ducks, swans, or geese. In fact, it might seem hard to believe that they're even in the same order!

If you didn't know screamers were waterfowl, you might think that they were closely related to turkeys. They have short, chicken-like beaks that curve downward and end in a sharp hook. Their long toes have very little webbing between them, and their large wings have bony spurs that stick forward. Screamers use these spurs to fight off predators and rival birds.

Screamers hardly ever swim. Their long toes make it possible for them to walk on floating plants. As they move across the plants, they pluck off leaves and buds with their sharp beaks. When screamers are on land, they spend a lot of time eating grasses and seeds. At night, these birds don't rest near the water like many other kinds of waterfowl. They *roost* in trees, like turkeys. They don't quack or honk, either. They scream!

Screamers build delicate nests of sticks and reeds near, or even in, the water. Males and females take turns sitting on the eggs. Young screamers look almost exactly like young swans.

19

Ducks

FAMILY: Anatidae
COMMON EXAMPLE: African pygmy goose
GENUS AND SPECIES: *Nettapus auritus*
SIZE: 13 inches (33 cm)

With its green, black, white, and reddish feathers, and its rich yellow beak, the African pygmy goose is one of the prettiest waterfowl in the world. But don't be fooled by its name. The African pygmy goose isn't really a goose. It's a duck. In fact, it's the smallest duck in Africa.

Despite their bright coloring, African pygmy geese can be hard to spot. In the daytime, they sit quietly in small groups, hiding among the water lilies. In the morning and evening, they swim about and eat water-lily seeds. Their strong, pointed bills are tailor-made for cracking these seeds. Every so often, they dive for insects and small fish.

African pygmy geese are graceful swimmers, but they're clumsy on land. They spend most of their time in the water. Sometimes they *perch* on a floating branch, but most of the time they use their webbed feet for swimming.

These little ducks mate during the wet season. They usually make their nests in tree holes, but sometimes they use other birds' nests. They may even nest in the thatched roof of someone's house. During the dry season, the ponds they live in may dry up. Then the African pygmy geese search for a bigger lake with plenty of water lilies. Anything's better than waddling about on land!

21

Ducks

FAMILY: Anatidae
COMMON EXAMPLE: Common shelduck
GENUS AND SPECIES: *Tadorna tadorna*
SIZE: 27 inches (68.5 cm)

It is early spring. Hundreds of common shelducks are returning from their winter homes in the south. The noise is nearly deafening. The males whistle and wheeze to the females, and the females answer, "Ga-ga-ga-ga-ga-ga-gak!"

Soon the shelducks pair off and wander away to look for a good place to build a nest. They may have to go far from the water to find just the right spot. They usually build nests in tree holes, in stream banks, or in rabbit holes. Sometimes they nest in haystacks or in an old dog house.

As soon as the ducklings hatch, their parents lead them to the water. It is time for the birds to meet up with the rest of the flock. The ducklings patter along the muddy shore, dabbling for shellfish, insects, and water weeds.

Soon the adult shelducks begin to *molt*. They lose their old feathers and grow new ones. A few adults stay with the ducklings, but most fly off to mud flats far from shore. The birds can't fly while they are molting. Being out on the mud flats helps them avoid predators. There's safety in numbers, too. In one place off the coast of Germany, as many as 100,000 common shelducks gather on the mud flats every year!

23

Ducks

FAMILY: Anatidae
COMMON EXAMPLE: Yellow-billed duck
GENUS AND SPECIES: *Anas undulata*
SIZE: 20 to 23 inches (51 to 58 cm)

It is early morning in Africa, and a huge flock of yellow-billed ducks is just waking up. They *preen* their feathers and shake them out. It's time for breakfast!

The yellow-bills paddle out onto the lake. They tip their tails up toward the sky and stick their heads underwater. This is how yellow-bills hunt for food. Stems and roots are tasty, and seeds, too. Water insects are always welcome. And they won't pass up small fish or tadpoles, either. They even eat small frogs.

The ducks spend the early morning hours feeding—paddling and dabbling, paddling and dabbling. But when the hot sun starts beating down, they head for a shady spot near the edge of the lake and spend the rest of the day loafing. When the sun begins to set, the ducks head out into the lake for dinner.

In the rainy season, the flock breaks up. Mated pairs fly away together to search for the perfect nesting spot. They look for flooded grasslands or a slow-flowing river with thick undergrowth along its banks. These ducks are picky about their nest sites. They may fly up to 600 miles (965 km) to find the ideal spot!

Geese

FAMILY: Anatidae
COMMON EXAMPLE: Greylag goose
GENUS AND SPECIES: *Anser anser*
SIZE: 35 inches (89 cm)

A greylag goose looks very familiar, and it should. It is the ancestor of the *domestic* geese you may have seen on a farm. Greylags are so heavy that they have to run along the ground for a stretch before they can lift off into the air. They use their strong, stout bills to tear tough leaves and stems off plants and dig up roots.

A flock of greylags can be very noisy. At the slightest sign of danger, they sound the alarm with loud, harsh honks. Their nasal calls sound like those of domestic geese, "Aahng-ahng-ung!" over and over. If you get too close to a greylag goose, it may feel threatened. It will honk loudly and run at you with its head down.

Greylags spend most of the year in large, noisy flocks. But at nesting time, males and females pair off and leave the flock to build a nest. Even though greylag nests are large, they can be hard to spot. They're usually hidden in the reeds at the edge of a pond or lake.

At one time, it seemed as though greylags were in danger of extinction. Some people were hunting them, and others were draining their water-y homes. But greylag geese are protected now, and they are making a comeback.

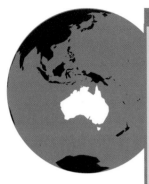

Ducks

FAMILY: Anatidae
COMMON EXAMPLE: Plumed whistling duck
GENUS AND SPECIES: *Dendrocygna eytoni*
SIZE: 24 inches (61 cm)

Plumed whistling ducks are a noisy bunch. If you hear them, you will understand how they get their name. They twitter constantly, giving out shrill whistles every few seconds: "Twitter twitter WACHEW! WACHEW! twitter twitter."

Unlike most ducks, plumed whistling ducks don't like to swim. At night they gather in huge flocks out in open grasslands and patter about feeding on seeds and grasses.

At daybreak, they fly to the shores of a lake. They spend the day napping in tightly packed groups. In the evening, they fly back to their feeding grounds. The lake where plumed whistling ducks roost and the grasslands where they eat may be as much as 35 miles (56 km) apart. During the dry season, the grasslands dry up. Then the birds fly to marshes and feed on plants called sedges and rushes.

Unlike most ducks, plumed whistling ducks mate for life. At the beginning of the rainy season, the flock breaks up into pairs. Each pair flies away to build a nest near water. Often, the ducks travel many miles to find just the right place. The nest is nothing fancy—just a scraped-out spot under a bush. When the ducklings hatch, their mother leads them to grasslands and teaches them to forage for food.

Ducks

FAMILY: Anatidae
COMMON EXAMPLE: Musk duck
GENUS AND SPECIES: *Biziura lobata*
SIZE: male 27 inches (68.5 cm); female
    21.5 inches (53 cm)

A musk duck is a strange looking bird. Its feathers are dark and oily-looking. It has a huge, round lobe hanging down from its chin. If you ever get close to a musk duck, you will find that they smell strange, too. Musk ducks get their name from the musky smell of their feathers.

These ducks spend most of their time in the water. They swim very low, with just the top of their back and their head showing. They're excellent divers, and they can stay underwater for a long time. Every so often, the ducks pop up to the surface, catch their breath, and then dive back down in search of tasty insects, fish, and frogs.

Musk ducks are usually quiet birds, but not during the breeding season. Full-grown males are much larger than females, and they put on noisy displays. Each male spreads his tail over his back and stretches his neck to show off the lobe on his chin. He turns around and around, kicking and splashing the water. At the same time, he grunts loudly and gives out loud shrill whistles. The females find all this very attractive!

After the ducks mate, the female builds a nest among the reeds at the water's edge. The male swims around nearby, ready to drive away anyone who dares to get too close.

Ducks

FAMILY: Anatidae
COMMON EXAMPLE: Northern shoveler
GENUS AND SPECIES: *Anas clypeata*
SIZE: 17 to 20 inches (43 to 51 cm)

The northern shoveler is an odd-looking duck. It has an oversized bill shaped like a spatula. Have you ever seen a flock of these birds swimming along with their big bills just under the water's surface? They were using their bills to strain bits of food out of the water.

Northern shovelers spend their winters in the south, where they begin to pair up for the mating season. This *courting* continues as the birds migrate north. When the ducks land, a group of males gathers around a female as she swims along. Each male tries to lead the female away from the others by swimming or flying a short distance away. Finally, the female chooses a male and flies off with him.

After the birds mate, the female builds a nest of grass and lines it with down. Then she sits on the eggs until they hatch. This may take as long as 4 weeks, but shoveler mothers don't seem to mind! As soon as the ducklings hatch, their mother leads them to the water. She tries to keep the ducklings hidden in the weeds, so hungry foxes won't see them. It doesn't take long for the ducklings to learn how to shovel up plant bits, snails, insects, and crayfish with their big bills.

Ducks

FAMILY: Anatidae
COMMON EXAMPLE: King eider
GENUS AND SPECIES: *Somateria spectabilis*
SIZE: 22 inches (56 cm)

King eiders must like the cold! They live in the far north, above the Arctic Circle, all year long. They spend most of their time hunting for food in the cold ocean waters. They like mussels and other shellfish best, but they also eat squid, fish, sand dollars, and even prickly sea urchins. King eiders can dive very deep. Some have been caught in fishing nets 150 feet (45 m) below the surface! When they're not busy feeding, they may hitch a ride on a passing *ice floe*.

In June, the flock breaks up. King eiders fly off two-by-two to raise their families on the tundra. The male's orange and black bulging forehead gets even bigger and brighter. He courts the female by crooning softly to her, "ahOOoo, ahOOoo."

Once the ducks have mated, the female lays eggs and sits on them. The male flies off to molt with other males. These flocks of molting birds can be enormous. On the coast of Greenland, 100,000 eiders gather at a time.

King eiders live so far north that they don't have to worry about people destroying their habitat or hunting them for food. Even though oil spills are a big problem for these birds, millions of eiders still live in the freezing Arctic waters.

Ducks

FAMILY: Anatidae
COMMON EXAMPLE: Mallard
GENUS AND SPECIES: *Anas platyrhynchos*
SIZE: 23 inches (58 cm)

Just about everyone knows what a mallard looks like. There are more mallards in the world than any other species of duck—nearly 10 million in North America alone! You can spot them in just about any marsh or pond, including ponds in city parks.

Mallards use their bills to strain all kinds of different foods out of the water. They eat seeds, leaves, insects, and worms near the surface. They tip themselves over to reach weeds and insects in the mud. In fall and winter, some mallards visit farms to gobble up seeds and corn kernels. Mallards in city ponds will eat any bits of bread you toss their way.

In the spring, you may see mallards courting. At mating time, the male is brightly colored. His head is green and his breast is purplish brown. The female follows behind the male, flicking her bill back over her shoulder. "Quegegegegege!" she calls. The male turns the back of his head toward her and swims slowly away. "Come with me!" he's saying.

Finally, the ducks turn to face each other. Each one lifts a wing and fans it out to show off the blue feathers on top: "Let's be mates!" Before long, the female will build her nest and lay eight to ten eggs. Soon there will be even more mallards dabbling in the pond!

Geese

FAMILY: Anatidae
COMMON EXAMPLE: Canada goose
GENUS AND SPECIES: *Branta canadensis*
SIZE: 45 inches (114 cm)

Out in a marsh in late winter, a female Canada goose makes her nest. She stands in the shallow spot she has hollowed out and stretches out her long neck to gather sticks, grass, and moss. Then she settles down to lay her eggs.

Meanwhile, her mate is busy defending the nest. Whenever another male gets too close, he stretches out his neck and waves his head back and forth. "Ahonk! Ahonk!" he yells at the intruder. If all this isn't enough to scare the other duck, the male pumps his head up and down. Then he attacks! He runs at the intruder with his neck stretched forward, hissing loudly. He's ready to fight for his *territory*!

As soon as the stranger runs away, the male runs over to his mate, and they greet each other like long-lost friends. He holds his neck down low and gives a call that sounds like a snore. Then he rolls his head back and forth, calling out " Ahonk! Ahonk!" The female stretches out her neck and answers, "Hink hink!" The pair creates a perfect duet. Their song sounds like one bird calling: "Ahonk!" "Hink!" "Ahonk!" "Hink!"

Swans

FAMILY: Anatidae
COMMON EXAMPLE: Mute swan
GENUS AND SPECIES: *Cygnus olor*
SIZE: 60 inches (152 cm)

All swans are elegant, but the mute swan may be the most beautiful and graceful of all. Its feathers are as white as snow, and its beak is black and red. This swan arches its wing feathers and holds its neck in a gentle curve as it glides across the water.

On land, the mute swan is not so graceful. Its legs are set far back on its body. This is great for swimming, but not for walking. Because the mute swan is so slow and awkward on land, it never goes very far from the water.

Like other swans, mute swans mate for life. They build their big mounded nests on small islands, hidden in the reeds. Soon after the cygnets hatch, you may see their mother swimming along with a baby swan on her back. The male guards his family fiercely. If an intruder comes near the nest, he swims at the enemy with jerky movements. He arches his wing feathers and holds his neck back on his shoulders. Most intruders get the message quickly!

As you might guess from their name, mute swans don't have a lot to say. Although they are silent most of the time, they do hiss and grunt when they are angry. And at breeding time, they snort. In the air, a flock of mute swans is very loud. A swan's wings make a throbbing whine as it flaps its wings. A flock of flying swans sounds like a small plane passing overhead.

Watching Waterfowl

Would you like to learn more about waterfowl? Because they are so large and many species are comfortable with people, they are among the easiest birds to watch. Before you head off to a nearby pond or marsh, gather a few items to help you enjoy the birds you see.

The most important tool is a pair of binoculars. Most birdwatchers like 10 × 40 binoculars. They make a bird look ten times larger. You'll also want a field guide to help you identify the birds you see. Field guides show pictures of the birds and point out each bird's most noticeable *field marks*, or features. Birds are often too small and too far away to see clearly, so knowing the shape of their bodies, the color of their bills, or the patterns on their feathers can help you identify them. Field guides also tell you what kinds of calls each bird makes. Finally, you will need a notebook to keep track of what you see. You can draw pictures of the waterfowl, and write down when and where you see them and how they behave.

As you get near a pond or marsh, walk quietly and slowly. You don't want to scare away any waterfowl that may be there. When you see a bird, keep your eyes on it while you raise your binoculars. Then take a good look. How big is the bird? What color is it? What special markings does it have? Check your field guide to find out what kind of bird it is.

Keep watching to see what the bird does. How does it feed? Does it stay in the water or walk about on land? Does it like to be alone or does it flock together with other birds? You may even see birds courting or young waterfowl swimming along behind their mother.

The more you watch and listen to birds, the more you'll know about them. And if you keep on watching the birds around you, you could become a real bird expert!

Words to Know

class—a group of creatures within a phylum that share certain characteristics.

courting—a series of actions intended to attract a mate.

cygnet—a baby swan.

dabbling—feeding on the surface of the water.

domestic—living with or near humans.

down—the soft, fluffy feathers below a bird's top layer of feathers.

extinct—no longer existing. Species may become extinct if they cannot adapt to their environment.

family—a group of creatures within an order that share certain characteristics.

field mark—a unique characteristic used to identify an animal.

forage—to look for and gather food.

genus (plural **genera**)—a group of creatures within a family that share certain characteristics.

gosling—the name for a baby goose.

habitat—the natural environment of an animal or plant.

ice floe—a large sheet of ice that has broken off an iceberg.

kingdom—one of the five categories into which all living things are placed: the animal kingdom, the plant kingdom, the fungus kingdom, the moneran kingdom, and the protist kingdom.

migration—a journey many birds make in the fall and spring.

molt—to shed or cast off an old layer of hair, skin, or feathers.

order—a group of creatures within a class that share certain characteristics.

ornithologist—a scientist who studies birds.

patter—to run with quick, light steps.

perch—to rest on a branch, rock, or other object.

phylum (plural **phyla**)—a group of creatures within a kingdom that share certain characteristics.

predator—an animal that hunts and eats other animals.

preen—to clean feathers with a bill or beak.

roost—to nest or sleep together.

species—a group of creatures within a genus that share certain characteristics. Members of a species can mate and produce young.

territory—the area an animal claims as its own. An animal hunts, sleeps, mates, and raises young within its territory.

tundra—a flat, treeless plain in regions close to the North Pole.

Learning More

Books

Burton, Jane and Angela Royston. *See How They Grow: Duck*. New York: Dutton, 1991.

Loomis, Jennifer A. *A Duck in a Tree*. Owings Mills, MD: Stemmer House, 1996.

Madge, Steven and Hillary Burn. *Waterfowl: An Identification Guide to the Ducks, Geese, and Swans of the World*. Boston: Houghton Mifflin, 1986.

Walton, Richard K. *North American Waterfowl*. Audubon Pocket Guides. New York: Knopf, 1994.

Zeaman, John. *Birds: From Forest to Family Room*. Danbury, CT: Franklin Watts, 1999.

Videos and CD-ROMs

Loons to Gamebirds. (Vol. 1; Guide to North American Birds series). The National Audubon Society.

Peterson Multimedia Guide to North American Birds. Houghton Mifflin Interactive.

Web Sites

Peterson Online

http://www.petersononline.com/birds/index.html

This site will help you identify North American waterfowl.

The Virtual Birder

http://magneto.cybersmith.com/vbirder/

Whether you are just starting out or are already a seasoned pro, this site has information that will interest you.

Index

About the Author

Sara Swan Miller has enjoyed working with children all her life, first as a Montessori nursery-school teacher, and later as an outdoor environmental educator at the Mohonk Preserve in New Paltz, New York. As the director of the Preserve school program, she has led hundreds of children on field trips and taught them the importance of appreciating and respecting the natural world.

She has written a number of children's books, including *Three Stories You Can Read to Your Dog; Three Stories You Can Read to Your Cat; What's in the Woods? An Outdoor Activity Book; Oh, Cats of Camp Rabbitbone!; Piggy in the Parlor and Other Tales; Better Than TV;* and *Will You Sting Me? Will You Bite? The Truth About Some Scary-Looking Insects.* She has also written many other books in the Animals in Order series.